If You're Not Growing, You're Dying: 7 Habits for Thriving in Your Faith, Relationships and Work

by Jon Beaty

Mustard Seed Imprints™

If You're Not Growing, You're Dying: 7 Habits for Thriving in Your Faith, Relationships and Work

By Jon Beaty

First Print Edition

Copyright © 2016, Mustard Seed Imprints

Published by
Mustard Seed Imprints
P.O. Box 1138
Estacada, Oregon 97023

Disclaimer

The information in this book without any express or implied warranty of any kind, including warranties of merchantability, noninfringement of intellectual property or fitness for any particular purpose. In no event shall the author, publisher or their agents or associates be liable for any damages whatsoever (including, without limitation, damages for loss of profits, business interruption, loss of information, injury or death) arising out of the use of or inability to use the information, even if has been advised of the possibility of such loss or damages.

All health and health-related information contained within this book is intended to be general in nature and should not be used as a substitute for a visit with a healthcare professional. The advice is intended to offer only a general basis for individuals to discuss their medical condition with their healthcare provider. A trusted healthcare provider should be consulted regarding matters concerning any medical condition and treatment for such conditions.

Links to external sites may be affiliate links for which the author or Mustard Seed Imprints may receive compensation for purchases made. The author or publisher cannot guarantee the accuracy of information found at any linked site. Links to or from external sites not owned or controlled by the author or publisher of this book, and do not constitute an endorsement of any employees of the sponsors of these sites or the products or information presented therein.

Contents

For Tami.

I love you more each day.

Start Here - How to Avoid the Destiny of Fools

Fools are destroyed by their own complacency.

Proverbs 1:32

You're designed to thrive.

The problem is most people aren't thriving in their faith, relationships and work. Some don't want to. Many don't know how. Frustrated by their lack of know-how, many give up and settle for a mediocre life. They lose their passion. They become complacent.

Settling for complacency can happen without even being aware you're settling. I was 40 years old when I realized I'd settled for a mediocre life. I'd been living that way for over a decade. I spent the next 8 years climbing out of the rut I'd slipped into.

I made a few wrong turns along the way. I also learned some valuable lessons. I can help you avoid those wrong turns. I can teach you what I've learned. That's the purpose of this book. By practicing what you learn in this book, you can begin a thriving life today–a life powered by faith, energized by love, and motivated by purpose.

A Thriving Faith

God designed you to have a thriving faith–faith that has the power to move mountains.

A thriving faith has substance. It's more than attending a church, giving to charities, or getting warm, fuzzy feelings when you hear your favorite praise song. A thriving faith enables you to see beyond the struggles, disappointments, and doubts of today. A thriving faith is an impenetrable shield, able to defend you against temptation and discouragement.

If you don't know how to grow a faith that works like that, this book is for you.

Thriving Relationships

God designed you to love and be loved.

We all want to belong. But some feel like they're the ones doing all the loving and getting nothing in return. You're running on empty, or very close to it. Thriving relationships are within your reach. You can love and be loved in return. You can love those who don't love you back. You can even love those who hurt and hate you. You can belong to something greater than yourself.

Is it really possible to love like that? Is it really possible to be loved? Your cup of love can be overflowing. This book tells you how.

Thriving at Work

I used to wonder why people work when they don't have to. You know, the millionaires and billionaires that could sit on a tropical beach for the rest of their life and drink lemonade–they keep working. Why?

God designed you to work.

Yes, work is hard. But work doesn't have to be meaningless. You don't have to dread Mondays. God wants your work to matter–to mean something. When your work has purpose, you want to show up. You want to give your best. You stop watching the clock, and start dreaming of the possibilities.

You no longer need to feel like you're in the wrong job, like you missed your calling, or that you're burned out. This book will reveal to you how to reignite your passion for your profession.

The Slow Road to Hell

To thrive means to grow.

If you're not growing in your faith, relationships and work, you're dying.

That might sound extreme. But it's true. Anyone who tells you something different isn't helping you. If you believe anything different, you're holding yourself back from being fully alive.

We can pretend there is a middle ground. It's called complacency. But the middle ground doesn't exist in reality. It's the slow road to hell.

Jesus warned against the wide gate that leads to destruction. Many take that path because it's easier to find. It's the path of least resistance. You can't thrive without resistance. The narrow gate leads to life, and few people find it. (Matthew 7:13-14). It's the path that builds the strength and endurance needed for a thriving life.

Complacency is the wide gate. It's your enemy–satisfaction with the status quo, with no desire to make things better, no concern that things could be getting worse.

Complacency tells you, "Maybe someday." Someday is always a day too late.

It can be easy to talk the talk. We tell ourselves and others, "Someday I'm going to do this, or do that." It's harder to walk the walk. Death comes to those who wait. Growth requires effort. Like a sprouting plant beneath a layer of asphalt, it slowly pushes, building its strength until it breaks through, out of the darkness, into the light.

If we neglect to feed our faith, we lose our power. We'll starve spiritually.

If we fail to pursue greater intimacy with God, and in our human relationships, we'll feel empty and alone, even when we're with other people.

If we don't continue to develop the skills and knowledge we need for our work, we'll disengage and burn out.

It's Time to Grow

Perhaps you've lost your way and you're looking for the road that leads you back to a better life. Maybe you never got on the right road to start with.

Some people start out lost and stay there to see where it leads. Maybe you didn't even know you had options to choose from–that makes it harder to find your way.

Don't fall for the lie that just because you're on a road that you're going somewhere worth going. Don't fall for the trap that you're stuck on the road you're on.

That's the trap of complacency.

If you don't know where the road goes, pull over and get answers. Ask questions. Learn from others who've gone that way. But don't just keep going. If you feel stuck on the road you're on, stop and ask for help to find the nearest exit.

By opening this book and reading every page, you can choose to not let your destiny be a matter of chance or ignorance. A life lived on the tides of circumstances is the life of an unfortunate fool. Ignorance isn't bliss–it's the highway to disappointment, destruction and a meaningless death.

With this book, you now have a map to show you how to thrive in your faith, relationships and work.

It's time for you to grow.

Begin with Habit 1 and work your way through one habit at a time. Set aside 10 minutes a week for the next 7 weeks, and review one habit each week. Commit to act on each new habit for a full week. This will help you make each habit a part of who you are. This will help you grow.

Growth is the life that God wants for you.

Live to Thrive!

Jon Beaty
Your Life Coach
www.jonbeaty.com

P.S. Nobody thrives in isolation. You and I both need to surround ourselves with people who want to live to thrive. A good place to start is by joining my exclusive "Alive to Thrive" tribe. Enter this URL in your internet browser now to claim your free membership and other bonuses: **jonbeaty.com/bonuses**

Habit 1 - Receive God's Love: 5 Simple Steps to Quench Your Spiritual Thirst

When the poor and needy search for water and there is none, and their tongues are parched from thirst, then I, the LORD, will answer them. I, the God of Israel, will never abandon them.

Isaiah 41:17

I was born to church-going parents who taught me about God at an early age.

One of my favorite children's books was a thick volume of Bible stories. I liked it because it had colorful, lifelike illustrations for each story. I could see Adam and Eve surrounded by all kinds of animals in the Garden of Eden, Noah watching animals enter the ark two by two, and Jesus healing broken people as crowds pressed in around Him.

One of those Bible stories included an illustration of Moses leading thousands of Hebrews on a path opened by God between the churning waters of the Red Sea. Behind them Egypt's Pharaoh pursued them with his army—charioteers driving horse-drawn chariots.

You might be familiar with that story. But how familiar are you with what happened a few days afterward?

Let me first recap what happened in the familiar story.

Moses and his older brother Aaron had come to Pharaoh asking to lead the enslaved Hebrews on a journey into the wilderness to worship God. Pharaoh refused. God sent 10 plagues on Egypt to change Pharaoh's mind.

Pharaoh's nation in shambles, and his first born son dead, he sent the Hebrews away. But it didn't take long for Pharaoh to regret his decision. He sent his army after the Hebrews to bring them back.

When the Hebrews fled Pharaoh's kingdom, God went ahead of them cloaked in a column of clouds. They fled while the sun was still in the sky. As night fell, the Egyptian army neared. God moved behind the Hebrews, and the column of clouds became a fiery pillar. Its glowing flames and scorching heat held Pharaoh's army back long enough to give the Hebrews a head start on their escape, as God parted the waters and Moses led them through the Red Sea.

Pharaoh's army followed.

As the Hebrews reached safety above the water line on the other side of the sea, God unleashed the waters. Pharaoh's pursuing army perished beneath the waves.

Safe on the shore, the Hebrews celebrated their freedom. Four hundred and thirty years in Egypt, most of those years they suffered in slavery. Now they were free. Now they were on their way to the Promised Land.

Bitter Waters

Now we get to what happened a few days later. This story isn't as familiar. The celebration on the eastern shore of the Red Sea plays like a happy ending. But it wasn't the end.

Between the Red Sea and the Promised Land lay a wilderness–mostly desert. God led the way by day in the cloud-column. At night, God watched over them from the pillar of fire.

The Hebrews hiked for three days. On the third day, their water supply went dry. Their mouths dry with thirst, they searched for water.

They found water in a desert oasis. But as they scooped it into their mouths, bitterness forced them to spit it out.

It was unfit to drink.

The Hebrews started to worry. Would they die of thirst?

They complained. Did Moses bring them here to die?

All that God had done to get them out of Egypt–the 10 plagues, moving the Red Sea aside, the cloud-column that gave them shade in the heat of the day, and the fire-pillar that gave them light, protection and warmth at night...

Forgotten!

It's easy to do that. Our natural instinct is to see the negative, to listen to our fears, to look for danger. We do this to survive.

The covering of shade in the heat of day, the warmth and light in the night–it was there. But they didn't see it–didn't feel it. They saw the danger. They felt the thirst. Their canteens and cups had run dry.

If we focus too much on what's wrong, what's scary, what threatens our survival, we lose sight of what's right, beautiful and safe. Our focus fuels bitterness. We worry. We complain.

God's there, but we can't see Him. We can't feel Him. We thirst, we drink, but nothing satisfies.

Thirsting for Love

When my parents divorced I was 10 years old. I lost my sense of security. I lost my home and my friends. I no longer felt loved. My thoughts turned negative. I avoided making new friends, fearing the pain of losing them again. I retreated to an imaginary world of science fiction novels and fantasy.

When I was 5, our family stopped attending church. Not long after that, we wandered away from God. After my parents' divorce, Dad searched for meaning, purpose and peace. As Dad searched, he noticed God walking alongside him and followed Him back to church.

A year after the divorce, Mom turned me and my younger brother Tyler over to Dad. A year later, Dad moved us from Mission Viejo, California, to Medford, Oregon, where we lived with Grandma and Grandad Beaty. We stayed there until Dad could buy us a house. It didn't take long, and we moved to a 900-square-foot home in

Jacksonville, an historic gold-mining town few miles west of Medford.

A few years later, an evangelist named Phil Schultz showed up at the church Tyler and I attended with Dad. We attended his meetings.

Pastor Schultz presented his messages in plain words that my 15-year-old brain could understand. I saw in greater detail than ever before how God loves me, what Jesus Christ did for me, and God's plan for my future. I began to see the positive in life. My fears began to subside. I felt a sense of safety.

Pastor Schultz made calls at the end of his meetings for people to take a stand for Jesus. I wanted to take a stand, but I was too shy to stand up in front of everyone.

Pastor Schultz paid a visit to our home one evening. He sat on a couch next to me, and he asked me if I wanted to follow Jesus and be baptized. His direct appeal to me to make a choice was all I needed.

A few weeks later, I stood in the warm waters of the baptismal pool in front of the church, behind the pulpit. Charles Byrd, the pastor of the church stood alongside me. He raised his right hand and shouted, "I now baptize you in the name of the Father, the Son and the Holy Spirit." With his left arm around my shoulders, his right hand held a cloth over my mouth and nose as he buried me in the water. Like the Hebrews escaping from slavery in Egypt through the waters of the Red Sea, I was freed from slavery to sin in the waters of that baptistery. When Pastor Byrd lifted me back to my feet, I rose from the water, my feet planted on the shores of a new life.

After my baptism, I had some spiritual nurturing at home, in the Christian school I attended, and in church services. But somehow I missed the importance of cultivating my own spiritual growth through daily prayer and Bible study. It's possible someone encouraged me to do daily devotions, but no one checked on me to see how I was growing.

God's love was still there, but I lost sight of it. God offered it, but I wasn't receiving it.

The peace I felt after I was baptized faded. After a while, I was running on empty. Worries piled up. Loneliness. Complaints. I felt thirsty–thirsty for love.

So, I looked for love in the wrong places. When I thought I'd found it, I discovered bitter waters.

What about you?

Quenching Your Thirst

We're all born with a thirst that can only be quenched by receiving God's love.

Here's the problem: When we look for love, like the Hebrews, we find bitter waters.

We may start from what seems like a disadvantage. But God pursues us like a lover in pursuit of his beloved.

You may have been born into a dysfunctional family, where love was lacking.

You may have been born into a home bursting with love. But even if your mother and father lavished you with love, it wasn't enough.

You may have found love, only to have your heart broken–more than once.

Whatever path your journey takes, you'll get thirsty for love, and find bitter waters.

It's because we look for love in the wrong places.

God's love always surrounds us. When we resist it, we die inside. To thrive, we must receive God's love daily. God's love nourishes our soul, causing us to grow, producing in us the fruit of the Spirit.

How do we receive God's love?

When the Hebrews found bitter waters, Moses did the best thing. He prayed.

Moses remembered what God had done in Egypt. Moses remembered the rescue at the Red Sea. Moses remembered God's promise of a new home for His people. Moses remembered God's love in action, and remembered His promises–that's what faith is. Moses felt God's love by faith.

Moses prayed, and God answered.

God showed Moses a tree. "Put it in the water," God said.

Moses did what was right. He obeyed God.

The tree touched the water, and the water became sweet.

God points you and me to a tree–the cross of Jesus Christ.

On the cross, love was made perfect. Love paid the penalty for our sin with its own life. That is the essence of true love–love that gives all that it has to heal what sin has broken–broken hearts, broken relationships and broken souls.

To receive God's love, pray. Ask for it. He's waiting to fill you with it. God wants to quench your thirst with the kind of love He gave at the cross.

Then give it away.

To continue receiving God's love we must give God's love.

To receive more of God's love, follow His directions. Do what He commands. He commands you to love. Give it away, and He'll give you more.

The more you give, the more you receive, until your cup runs over.

Because of the cross, love can transform you. Because of the cross, you can love. To love is to thrive!

When we receive God's love, as He displayed His love on the cross, Jesus makes our bitter waters sweet.

Jesus quenches our thirst with living water.

Love Overflowing

You might remember this story.

Jesus and a woman met at a well. She came to the well alone–a woman only went for water alone when she didn't have friends.

Jesus saw her empty, broken heart, and her need for love. She'd looked for love in the wrong places. Five men. Five attempts at making love last. Five times she found bitter waters.

Jesus offered her living water–water that would heal, and overflow with everlasting love.

All she had to do is ask and receive. When she received it, she went to share it with everyone she knew.

All we have to do is ask and receive, then give it away. Let the energy that's God's love flow in you and through you.

If you're thirsty for that kind of love, start taking these 5 simple steps, and keep on walking:

1. Believe by faith that God's love is always where you are.

Faith is believing that God keeps His Word. The Bible is reliable record of God's faithfulness. The apostle Paul believed it, when he wrote:

> "And I am convinced that nothing can ever separate us from God's love. Neither death nor life, neither angels nor demons, neither our fears for today nor our worries about tomorrow— not even the powers of hell can separate us from God's love." Romans 8:38

When the weeds of doubt pop up, pluck them out by reading this passage.

2. Pray when you can't see anything good, when you feel afraid, or when you begin to worry and complain.

Prayer is our hotline to God, and as powerful as God Himself.

> "Don't worry about anything; instead, pray about everything. Tell God what you need, and thank him for all he has done. Then you will experience God's peace, which exceeds anything we can understand. His peace will guard your hearts and minds as you live in Christ Jesus." Philippians 4:6-7

Talk to God anytime and anywhere in the privacy of your thoughts, by writing in a journal, or with spoken words.

3. Ask God to quench your thirst with His everlasting love.

When Jesus met the woman at the well, He offered to quench her thirst. The offer Jesus made to her is also available to you.

> "Jesus replied, 'Anyone who drinks this water will soon become thirsty again. But those who drink the water I give will never be thirsty again. It becomes a fresh, bubbling spring within them, giving them eternal life.'" John 4:13-14

When you feel alone, abandoned, or afraid, ask God to come near to you, to draw near to you, and to draw you close to Him.

4. Receive God's love, by remembering His blessings, and believing His promises.

Train your brain to focus on what is good, and run from the bad stuff:

> "Always be joyful. Never stop praying. Be thankful in all circumstances, for this is God's will for you who belong to Christ Jesus. Do not stifle the Holy Spirit. Do not scoff at prophecies, but test everything that is said. Hold on to what is good. Stay away from every kind of evil." 1 Thessalonians 5:16-22

End each day by writing down at least one thing that went well that day. Find Bible promises that speak to you, write them on notes where you'll see them frequently, and start putting them to memory.

5. Give love away.

Be generous with the love God has given you by sharing it with others

> "We know what real love is because Jesus gave up his life for us. So we also ought to give up our lives for our brothers and sisters."1 John 3:16

Start each day by choosing at least one person to be the recipient of a kind word or action, delivered by you.

Then do it all again. Live to thrive!

Habit 2 - Appreciate God's Gifts: 3 Life-Changing Benefits of Gratitude

In every thing give thanks: for this is the will of God in Christ Jesus

concerning you.

1 Thessalonians 5:18

My freshman year at Walla Walla University I enrolled as a recreation major.

Yes, that was a real major.

I'd just come off my first summer as a camp counselor at Big Lake Youth Camp. The camp is hidden in evergreen forest at the base of Mt. Washington, near Sisters, Oregon. That summer was the best summer I'd ever had. For 8 weeks in a row, I welcomed a fresh batch of teenage boys into my cabin. I'd mentor them and enjoy activities like sailing, archery, and mountain biking. With an education in recreation, I dreamed of a career working in a youth center. It would be like working at summer camp year round.

I Needed a Job

To get through college I needed a job. Coach Windemuth was my academic advisor, and hired me to work for him. My job title was "uniform attendant." My job was to manage the uniforms used in the university's intramural sports program. I'd check the uniforms out to the students for each evening's games, then collect, wash and re-hang them when the games were over.

In the spring I got a second job. The facility manager for the physical education department hired me to wash the tennis courts. Each Friday I'd roll out a fire hose and spend a few hours spraying the dirt off the courts that had collected during the week. It turned out to be a good way to get a tan.

These jobs didn't compare to working at camp, though. I planned to return to Big Lake Youth Camp the next summer. In the spring, I expected to receive a letter confirming my employment. When my friend Doug received his letter, anxiety built up each day after that as I checked my mailbox and didn't receive mine.

As weeks went by, the more I worried I wouldn't be invited back to camp. Doug insisted I call Gary, the camp director, and find out what was going on. So I did.

Gary told me he wasn't sure he wanted to rehire me. He thought I lacked energy and enthusiasm. He wasn't sure I enjoyed working at camp.

On the Verge of Loss

When you're an introvert who doesn't wear his or her emotions for everyone to see, that bothers people who rely on seeing emotions for a sense of what others are thinking. That's the predicament I'd gotten myself into. Gary was a high-energy extrovert with contagious enthusiasm. It troubled him that his enthusiasm hadn't infected me.

What Gary didn't know was that I was enthusiastic. I just didn't show it the way he wanted. I did have energy. But I was an endurance runner not a sprinter.

I promised to change my ways. Doug even vouched for me. Gary gave me a chance to prove myself, and invited me back to camp.

I didn't yet understand the power of gratitude. But since that time I've learned that nothing gives gratitude more power than realizing something you value could be lost or taken away.

I returned to camp a little more extroverted. I shouted, cheered, clapped and sprinted with best of them. Gary acknowledged my "improvement." I thanked him for the opportunity. The experience stretched me, and I had a good time. I could have complained about being pushed to act in a way that wasn't natural for me. Instead, I savored my camp experience knowing that I almost missed out on it.

Trouble with the Law

When the camp season ended, I returned to Walla Walla for my sophomore year. The jobs I'd held the year before, and my summer camp job, didn't put cash in my wallet. Paychecks for on-campus jobs were deposited in my student account to pay down my tuition, room and cafeteria expenses. I wanted a job that allowed me to put some cash in my wallet. I needed cash to gas up my car and for extracurricular activities with friends.

I interviewed for a job delivering pizzas for Domino's. They hired me on the spot.

One evening I had a delivery to the women's dormitory on the university campus. Thinking I'd save some time, I parked my Mazda GLC in an open parking space along the street outside the dorm. I set the parking brake, and left my car idling while I ran the pizza to the dorm's front desk.

As I jogged back to my car, a police car's flashing lights let me (and everyone else) know I'd gotten a police officer's attention. The officer stood in front of my car, writing a ticket. To my surprise, I learned it's illegal to leave a car running unattended on a public road. It was worth a fine of something like a hundred and ten dollars.

A few weeks later I appeared in traffic court with a room full of college students. The judge called my name.

I'd thought about pleading "not guilty." But I was smart enough to know that ignorance of the law wasn't enough to clear me of my guilt. At best, I hoped admitting my ignorance might win me some leniency–I was a college student on a tight budget. So, I pled guilty, and briefly explained my ignorance. The judge had mercy on me, and lowered my fine to about fifty dollars.

Ignorance Isn't Bliss

My experience in traffic court reminds me that not knowing about a law doesn't release us from the consequences of not obeying it. If you climb on your roof to replace missing shingles, you will slip and fall if you lose your footing. The law of gravity assures the outcome, even if you don't know the law exists. Fortunately, we learn to respect the law of gravity at an early age.

Like the well-known law of gravity, I believe there is a law of gratitude. But unlike the law of gravity, the law of gratitude is often forgotten.

In 1 Thessalonians 5:18, the Apostle Paul wrote:

> In every thing give thanks: for this is the will of God in Christ Jesus concerning you.

When you think of God's laws, His 10 Commandments are probably the first thing to come to mind. But there are other laws, such as the laws of physics. God didn't write these in granite for us, but we know they exist.

There are also laws of nature, put in place by God to assure certain outcomes when certain actions take place. Reproduction occurs, things grow, and things die according to the laws of nature. I think the law of gratitude is one of those natural laws.

Gratitude is the Best Attitude

God's laws always come with blessings or benefits, and the law of gratitude is no exception. Three of the greatest benefits are illustrated in the story of Jesus' encounter with 10 men infected with leprosy.

Headed south through Palestine, Jesus had walked through Samaria and came to Galilee. The Bible doesn't tell us if Jesus was traveling alone or with His disciples. But the context of the story in Luke 17 makes me believe they were with him.

The dusty road they traveled came to a village. On the outskirts of the village, Jesus and his disciples might have normally been met by curious children. But here they were met by 10 lepers.

The disfiguring effects of leprosy on their skin, causing sores on their faces, hands and feet, would have instilled fear in the other villagers. Their hideous appearance would've been hidden by whatever scraps of cloth the men had scavenged to wrap themselves with. But their apparel would have done nothing to make them accepted in the village. Because of their disease, the villagers would have required these men to keep a distance from the rest of the population.

As Jesus and his disciples walked toward them, out of shame the lepers kept their distance. But when they were close enough to be heard, they called out:

"Jesus, Master, have mercy on us."

It appears that Jesus responded immediately.

Luke writes in verse 14:

"He looked at them and said, 'Go show yourselves to the priests.' And as they went, they were cleansed of their leprosy."

The men obeyed, and were instantly healed.

For nine of those men, the law of gratitude was forgotten, perhaps even unknown. They would miss out on its benefits.

But one man paused long enough to notice what Jesus had done for him.

Where the man once saw disfigured hands with stubbed fingers extending from the sleeves of his tunic, he now saw new, soft, supple skin. His fingers were restored.

He once struggled to keep his balance while walking. He lacked feeling in what was left of his feet and toes. Now he felt a spring in his step.

He touched his face with his new fingers. If he could only see what he felt! His nose, chin, cheeks and lips were made whole again.

He turned back to Jesus. Praising God with a loud voice, he fell on his face at Jesus' feet. Overwhelmed with gratitude, the man gave thanks.

And Jesus said to him:

"Stand up and go. Your faith has healed you." Luke 17:19

Gratitude's Life-Changing Benefits

Did you notice the 3 benefits of gratitude experienced by this former leper? Here they are:

1. Gratitude makes us happier.

The former leper was so happy, he ran back to Jesus praising God. He was happier because he noticed and savored the gift.

We often overlook the blessings God has put in our path. Many of us have trained our brains to focus on the unsavory things and negative moments in life. There's a purpose for recognizing risks and seeing danger. It can protect us. But when we survive abuse, war, injury, loss, betrayal or other traumatic events, many of us begin to see risks and danger at every turn on life's journey.

Gratitude, sadness and fear can't occupy the same space. Gratitude enables us to push aside negative feelings.

2. Gratitude makes us less self-centered.

Unlike the nine men who didn't express gratitude, the man who did turned his focus from his self to Jesus.

Focus on self isolates us from the people around us and from God. Over time, a self-centered focus will sever our most important relationships. We'll end up alone.

Gratefulness turns our focus to the people around us and to God. We can't be grateful to ourselves. Gratitude turns our attention to the giver of whatever we're thankful for.

3. Gratitude helps us thrive.

The absence of illness isn't the same as thriving. To not be sick isn't the same as being well.

Of the 10 lepers that were healed, only one experienced what it means to thrive. Just being healed doesn't make one well. We can be healed, then get sick again.

Thriving depends on our ability to look outside ourselves. A focus inward will make us self-centered. Instead of standing tall and strong, bearing delicious fruit, we will bend over, weighed down by branches full of deformed, sour fruit, until we break under the strain.

Savoring what health we have as an opportunity to bless others–that's living to thrive.

Faith in the one who gives us healing, expressed through gratitude–that's living to thrive.

Develop the habit of gratitude by savoring your blessings, and writing them in journal 2 to 3 days a week. And when someone blesses you, whether it's God or someone else, say a sincere "thank you!"

Habit 3 - Purify God's Temple: Become a Healthier You

Don't you realize that your body is the temple of the Holy Spirit, who lives in you and was given to you by God? You do not belong to yourself, for God bought you with a high price. So you must honor God with your body.

1 Corinthians 6:19-20

I became a fat vegetarian.

When I was 4 years old, I'd walk with my Grandma Portillo to the butcher shop on Euclid Avenue. The shop was a few blocks from her home on Nina Place, in Garden Grove, California. Grandma was my daycare provider while Mom and Dad worked.

A bell would ring on the door whenever we entered the butcher's shop. The butcher wore a white paper service hat. He'd wipe his hands on his white, blood-stained apron and offer me a small lollipop from the Styrofoam cup he kept them in near his cash register. I always accepted. While I tore off the plastic wrapper and licked the fruity flavor of the lollipop, Grandma would order her beef steak. The butcher would chop a chunk meat with his cleaver, weigh it, then wrap it in white paper. Grandma would pay him with cash, then put the wrapped meat in the large carrying bag she brought with her. Then we'd walk back to her home.

Grandpa loved to barbecue a steak. Sometimes we'd visit Grandma and Grandpa on the weekend. Grandpa would tend the barbecue in the backyard, and Grandma would prepare coleslaw and potatoes.

When it came time to eat, we'd all sit around a long table on the modest, covered patio. The coleslaw and potatoes tasted good. But I always felt like I would choke on the charred meat. I'd chew and chew, but the bite in my mouth wouldn't get any smaller.

Grandma and Grandpa always provided the best desserts. Grandpa worked for Knudsen's Dairy and would bring home fresh ice cream. Grandpa also loved soft-serve ice cream. On warm summer evenings I'd sit between Grandma and Grandpa in the front seat of their 1968 Buick Skylark, and Grandpa would drive us to an ice cream parlor near Disneyland.

Disneyland was only a few minutes from my grandparents' house. When the sky got dark, a we'd see a bright spotlight shine on the top of Matterhorn mountain, and Tinker Bell would fly off its peak. As she descended into the night, a 20 minute fireworks display would fill the sky with color, smoke and noise. I'd watch in awe as I licked my vanilla ice cream from a crispy sugar cone.

A New Menu

After my parents divorced and my Dad moved me and my brother to Medford, Oregon. Grandma and Grandad Beaty introduced me to more nutritious food. They'd developed much of their half-acre lot into a thriving garden of greens, fruits, beans and potatoes.

In the summer that we lived with Grandma and Grandad, I was introduced to the taste of fresh produce, much of which I'd never tasted before. Except for the occasional trout or salmon Grandad hooked on his fishing trips, there was no meat served in their home. There were no dairy products. There was no refined sugar. I ate good, though. Grandma prepared delicious meals, including desserts she sweetened with dates or honey.

Grandma and Grandad ate this way because they read in the Bible that the body is a temple for the Holy Spirit.

The tabernacle in the wilderness that Moses built under God's direction was God's first temple on earth. Before entering the tabernacle, the priests were required to purify themselves at its entrance. They cleansed themselves by washing their hands and feet in the pure water of the bronze laver. The priests and tabernacle represented Jesus Christ, and God set them apart, or made them *holy* for that purpose.

God calls Christians to the same kind of holiness, as Jesus' representatives:

> "Now may the God of peace make you holy in every way, and may your whole spirit and soul and body be kept blameless until our Lord Jesus Christ comes again." 1 Thessalonians 5:23

We can't make ourselves holy. But by choosing to do what God instructs us to do, we receive His holiness (Acts 2:38).

In the Book of Daniel, the story of Daniel begins with his arrival in Babylon as a captive of King Nebuchadnezzar. Daniel was young, probably in his teens. He was among other young men who'd been brought to Babylon from Jerusalem, chosen for their connections to their nation's royal family to be trained in the language and literature of Babylon.

The young men were destined to serve in Nebuchadnezzar's government. He sought their loyalty. So he ordered that all the young men be fed meat and wine from the king's kitchen. Through the biblical books of Moses, God had provided His people with instructions in right living, including how to eat.

The nutritional guidance God gave to Moses for the Hebrews wasn't arbitrary. God designed humans to thrive. God set thriving as the default mode. But after Adam and Eve made the first poor nutritional choice in the Garden of Eden, the health of humanity began to decline. Death became the default. Thriving would occur only through a conscious choice to live the kind of life we were designed for.

God designed humans to thrive on a diet of fruits and vegetables (Genesis 1:29). After the Great Flood, God introduced "clean" animals into the diet of Noah and His family (Genesis 9:2; 7:3). Most land vegetation had been destroyed by the worldwide flood. But with the introduction of meat, the length of people's lives was reduced by hundreds of years. Before the flood, Methuselah lived 969 years. A few generations later, Abraham died at 175. Today, few people live past 100.

You can see the direction we're going. Recent research connects a diet rich in meat, or foods that have a high glycemic index, with early death. People who eat a diet high in plant-based foods have less disease and live longer.[1]

---

1 "Vegeterian Dietary Patterns and Mortality in Adventist Health Study 2," JAMA Internal Medicine, July 8, 2013, 172(13):30-1238
http://www.ncbi.nlm.nih.gov/pmc/articles/PMC4191896/

At least four of the young men recalled the nutritional lessons they learned in studying God's Word, and chose to do as God commanded. These young men were Daniel and his 3 friends, Hananiah, Mishael, and Azariah. Choosing to avoid the disease of mind and body that would come from consuming the king's meat and wine, they requested and received a diet of vegetables and water.

Daniel also proposed a test that might be the first recorded clinical study of the effects of nutrition. He proposed that after 10 days of eating their preferred diet, that the king's staff compare Daniel and his friends to the young men who'd dined on the king's best meat and sipped on the finest wine. After 10 days Daniel and the 3 other boys appeared healthier and better nourished (Daniel 1:15). Because of their choice to follow God's instructions, God set them apart to serve Him in Babylon.

There they thrived!

I Thought I Was Healthy

The photos show me putting on extra pounds during my wife's pregnancy. While Tami had a good reason to add weight, I didn't. As my waistline and neck expanded, I expanded my wardrobe to fit.

I didn't think much of my weight gain. I thought I was healthy. I'd chosen to avoid eating meat to be healthy. I'd eat fish, chicken and turkey a few times a year, but otherwise my diet was mostly processed foods.

My favorite "whole" foods were cheddar and jack cheese. I admit this, knowing that the mere mention of cheese might trigger your own cheese cravings. Cheese is addictive[2]. Too much of it will clog your arteries and make you fat. That's what happened to me. I loved pizza, cheese sandwiches, cheese omelets, nachos, macaroni and cheese, cheese lasagna...anything with cheese.

Breads and pasta took second place on my list of favorite foods. Fruit juice was my usual beverage. I thought of these as health foods. But their high glycemic index spikes your blood sugar. Eating and drinking foods and beverages with a high glycemic index can cause your body to store extra fat and lead to type 2 diabetes.

During my university years, I ran for exercise, and on the track team. Ten years later, my exercise was limited to an occasional hike on the weekend.

At 45 years old I was about 30 pounds overweight. My cholesterol count was high. My blood pressure was high. I was a fat vegetarian.

---

2 "Cheese really is crack. Study reveals cheese is as addictive as drugs," Los Angeles Times, October 22, 2015,
http://www.latimes.com/food/dailydish/la-dd-cheese-addictive-drugs-20151022-story.html

My doctor was concerned enough to offer me statins.

I started exercising to try to reverse the damage. But I needed more than exercise.

When our physical health suffers, our brain is put at risk. Our brain depends on a healthy flow of blood to supply our neurons with oxygen and the right balance of nutrients. Without a nourishing blood flow, our ability to think clearly, solve problems, and exercise good judgment is compromised. Blood sugar imbalances begin to do damage to the brain, leading to depression and increasing the risk of Alzheimer's dementia. Most people don't recognize the subtle changes in their brain functioning until it's too late.

In her last few years of life, my Grandma Portillo suffered from dementia. She lost her ability to make rational decisions. She lost her ability to recognize people. She began seeing, hearing, and believing things that were disconnected from reality. She couldn't understand anything about God's love for her. She mistook her family for strangers. She couldn't take care of herself and had to be cared for in an adult foster home.

Our brain is our only connection to God. Poor brain functioning can eventually sever our connection to God, and to the people we love. If our body is a temple for the Holy Spirit, our brain is the throne room where God gives guidance, and His messages are received.

Grandma's family continued to love her, and God did, too. But how tragic for her to live her final days in confusion and fear. If she'd known a way to avoid that kind of ending, I'm sure she would have chosen it.

You have a choice. Science is providing us with an increasing amount of evidence that tells us we can prevent many diseases doctors once thought were unavoidable. Diseases once thought to be incurable can be reversed. We can often prevent and reverse disease through simple lifestyle changes.

I made several, half-hearted attempts at improving my health over the years. The turning point came when I began to doze off at my work desk a few hours after eating. In my quest to discover what was going on, I discovered I had stage-4 pre-diabetes. It was the last stage before meeting the criteria for a type-2 diabetes diagnosis.

Diabetes is a life-changing disease. Unchecked, it affects the mind, and destroys the body. A poorly functioning brain and failing body cause relationships and work to suffer. I wasn't thriving. I was on the path towards a slow, meaningless death.

When truth leads you to a fork in the road, it's time to make a decision. Sometimes, we look around to see which path other people are taking. We follow the crowd, because it seems easier. But easier is often not best, and often leads to destruction.

The truth revealed I need a change in my nutrition and my lifestyle. When we choose to change, we're often choosing to go against the flow. Change is an uphill journey. But I chose it. I wanted to live.

7 Secrets to a Healthier You

When making a diagnosis, drugs are the first line of treatment recommended by many doctors. After doctors leave medical school, much of the continuing education they get is sponsored by pharmaceutical companies. It makes sense, then, that many doctors would choose drugs to treat the conditions their patients present with.

The appeal of a drug is that it's a "quick fix." Popping a pill each day seems easier than choosing the challenges of saying no to food that will kill you, getting better nutrition, becoming more active, and learning how to reduce and manage stress. Medications are easier in the short term, and may save you in a time of crisis. But medications usually aren't a cure, and seldom a good long-term solution. Poor nutrition, an unhealthy lifestyle, and drug side-effects will lead to an early death.

I rejected the conventional approach to treating my pre-diabetes with medication. I chose to reverse my pre-diabetes with the help of 7 secrets. I call them secrets, because they're unknown by most people. But history and a growing body of scientific evidence reveals these secrets work to stop the progress of many diseases and sometimes reverse it. They may be the secrets to a healthier you.

Ask God to give you the strength to overcome the challenges of change, going against the flow, and forming new habits. As you get started, I also recommend you consult with a trusted healthcare professional, who understands the power of nutrition and lifestyle to restore and improve health.

1. Nutrition

Build your meals on plant-based foods. Foods that don't have ingredient labels are the best to build a thriving body. These include greens, beans, berries, whole grains, nuts and seeds. Eat a full breakfast every day, and have your last meal of the day no less than 4 hours before bedtime.

If plant-based foods aren't available in sufficient amounts to meet your nutritional needs, consider supplementing your nutrition with scaled fish from clean waters, and poultry and meats from animals that have been well cared for, aren't diseased, and aren't treated with antibiotics and steroids.

2. Exercise

A combination of walking and strength building exercises is good for most people.

The best time for walking is immediately after eating. A 10-20 minute walk after eating helps keep blood sugars from spiking and prevents storage of unnecessary fat.

Strength building exercise helps strengthen your muscles and bones.

Adding interval training to your daily exercise can also increase your metabolism and help burn extra fat. Interval training alternates between walking or jogging at a moderate pace for 2 1/2 minutes then sprinting for 30 seconds.

3. Clean Water

Clean water used inside and outside of the body helps clean out dead cells, remove toxins, keeps skin soft, and prevents premature wrinkling.

How much water should you drink? Divide your body weight in pounds by half. The number you get is the minimum total number of ounces of water most people should drink throughout the day to stay well hydrated. So, if your weight is 200 pounds, 100 ounces of water a day is the amount of water needed to stay hydrated. It's usually best to drink no less than 30 minutes before eating and at least 90 minutes after eating to avoid diluting stomach acid used for digestion.

Daily bathing is also important. Need I say more?

To find out how clean your local water is you may be able to view a water quality report online, or request it from your local water utility. If you buy bottled water, you may be able to obtain a water quality report from the bottling company. If your water comes from a well, you may need to collect a sample and send it to a local lab that can test your water quality.

4. Sunlight

A minimum of 30 minutes a day in direct sunlight helps stimulate a better mood and stronger immune system. The best time for sunlight is early morning, shortly after waking. In some places the daylight hours get short in the winter. Overcast skies may block the sun's rays more days than not. If the sunlight is lacking, a lightbox may be necessary. A 10,000-lux light therapy lamp such as this one offered on Amazon (**http://amzn.to/1XKSPrK**) can help if you experience seasonal blues from a lack of sunlight.

Proper sunlight for 30 minutes each morning helps stimulate nighttime melatonin production. Melatonin is a naturally occurring hormone used by the brain to repair itself. It's also used to produce other hormones that help us manage stress, support positive moods, and boost immunity.

Sunlight is also important for vitamin D production. Low concentrations of vitamin D in the blood have been correlated with weakened immunity to viruses, an increased risk of cancer, and mental illness.

5. Temperance

Temperance isn't a word you'll hear often. Almost 200 years ago "temperance societies" were common in the United States and England. These groups were formed by men and women who'd pledged to abstain from alcohol.

Alcohol and drugs do significant damage to the human body. The reasoning power of the brain is weakened by alcohol and drugs, affecting a person's ability to use good judgment, control their behavior, and avoid dangerous situations.

While wine is often touted as a health food, it's also associated with an increased risk for cancer. Studies that show drinking wine lowers the risk of heart disease were done on people who eat meat[3]. Frequent meat eating is associated with an increased risk of heart disease. The wine cancels some of the adverse effects of frequent meat eating, but replaces those with other risks.

Caffeine is a drug that also damages the body when used excessively[4]. It passes quickly to the brain, and can lead to anxiety and depression, restlessness, heart palpitations, and tremors. If you wonder if your caffeine intake is too high, stop using it for a week and see what happens to your mind and body. If you experience withdrawal symptoms like headaches and irritability, nausea or vomiting, cutting back on caffeine might be in your best interests.

6. Fresh Air

Fresh air invigorates the mind and body. We need it to clean out the toxins that build up in our lungs. Breathing fresh air clears our mind and gives energy to our body. It lowers blood pressure, relieves tension, and improves our mood.

Fresh air has qualities that filtered indoor air lacks. Fresh air contains oxygen necessary for effective brain functioning, and negative ions that invigorate the mind and body.

If you work inside a building with windows that don't open, make a point of using your break time to step outside and breathe fresh air. If you work downtown in and urban area, take your break in a park, or near a water feature–there will be more negative ions there.

---

3 "Red Wine: Heart Healthy," Joel Fuhrman, M.D. https://www.drfuhrman.com/library/redwine.aspx/

4 "Caffeine in the Diet," MedlinePlus, United States National Institutes of Health. https://www.nlm.nih.gov/medlineplus/ency/article/002445.htm/

No fresh air around your workplace? Try at least part of your daily exercise in a place where there are green trees or shrubs, or along a natural stream, lake or ocean. These natural environments add to the quality of the air you breathe.

7. Rest

When we work more than 8 hours a day, 40 hours a week, the increase in our productivity is temporary[5]. After 8 hours, fatigue sets in. We slow down. We make mistakes. Our most productive work occurs between our second and sixth hours on the job. We might achieve a short-lived advantage, but after 2 weeks of overtime and overwork, safety is compromised, focus lost, judgment impaired, health compromised. After that, it only gets worse.

Take time to get 7-8 hours of sleep each day. God designed us to sleep at night, when it's dark. He also designed us to rest every seventh day. Rest is essential to thriving in faith, relationships and work.

Get Started Today

You can start creating a healthier you today. Apply each of these tips for 8 weeks, and you'll notice a positive difference in how you feel.

---

5 "Bring Back the 40 Hour Work Week," Sara Robinson, *Salon*, March 14, 2012.
http://www.salon.com/2012/03/14/bring_back_the_40_hour_work_week/

You'll also replace unhealthy habits with habits to help you thrive.

But remember this: Thriving health isn't an end in itself. It's one piece of a thriving life that enables us to share God's love with others and enjoy an abundance of gratitude.

Habit 4 - Consume God's Word: 4 Ways to Get Your Spiritual Superfood

In the beginning the Word already existed. The Word was with God,
and the Word was God.

John 1:1

Our first date was almost our last.

My wife and I met at Big Lake Youth Camp. I was 18. Tami was 16. The camp is a little piece of paradise tucked away among tall evergreens on the east bank of a clear, alpine lake in the Oregon Cascade Mountains. It sits along the Pacific Crest Trail that connects California, Oregon and Washington, about 20 minutes west of the small town of Sisters, at the foot of the jagged peak named Mt. Washington.

Tami and I worked on the summer camp staff. A week and a half before the summer camp season started, we arrived for staff orientation. We attended meetings to review camp policies, auditioned for and practiced plays that would provide evening entertainment and moral lessons for the kids, shoveled snow left over from the cold winter, and spread fresh wood chips on the ground to keep the dust down.

We hardly noticed each other. On the final Thursday of staff orientation, the camp director and kitchen staff hosted a staff banquet in the large dining hall of the camp lodge. To make things interesting, staff filled out a questionnaire that was used to pair guys and gals together for the banquet. The questionnaire asked about unimportant things like your favorite color and where you liked to vacation. This was before the World Wide Web and the dawn of online dating sites. But the answers were run through a simple computer program to match people together who gave similar answers.

Tami and I were matched.

Tami and I hadn't spoken to each other before our computer-matched date. I knew who she was. I'd seen her around camp, and had noticed her toothpaste-model smile, and playful, blue eyes. Her brunette, shoulder-length hair was done in a curly perm. I thought she was pretty, but she didn't strike me as my type.

When we sat down for dinner, we found we didn't have much in common beyond our answers to the silly questions on the questionnaire. Tami was a pastor's kid, and the only child of parents who loved each other. I was the oldest brother of two, and two more half-brothers. My parents were divorced from each other, and Mom had remarried. Tami was still in high school. She loved to talk, and looked forward to working as a staff substitute all summer, filling in for other staff on their days off. I had graduated from high school a few weeks before coming to camp, and planned to start college in the fall. I was a listener, more than a talker. I looked forward to working as a camp counselor, mentoring a new group of boys each week.

We didn't find each other very interesting.

Then She Caught My Eye

As the summer went on, our attention focused elsewhere. Tami hooked up with Ron, a dark-haired college sophomore. I fell for a pretty blonde, blue-eyed college sophomore named Donna.

Four years went by.

My relationship with Donna didn't last more than about 6 months. Her university was in Southern California. Mine was in Southeastern Washington. I returned to camp the next summer, and the next, and didn't notice Tami again until my fourth summer.

I'd only had one other girlfriend after Donna. I was shy with the ladies, and found it hard to muster up the courage to ask girls out.

When I did find the courage, it would set me back for several weeks when a request for a date was declined.

I was now an assistant camp director working in the camp office, and walking around camp to assure activities were operating on time. I was 22. Tami was now 20.

Tami started catching my eye in ways that she hadn't before.

On Sunday mornings we'd send the kids home who'd been at camp the week before. On Sunday afternoons, when a fresh batch of kids would arrive, I'd work in the office scheduling activities for the week ahead. Tami would help in the office with the registration of the new campers. So, we'd have time to chat when the influx of kids was slow.

One Sunday afternoon my friend Doug was in the camp office doing some paperwork. He suggested we take our day off together that week, invite a couple of girls, and make it a double date. He'd warmed up to a girl named Beki. He saw me watching Tami, and suggested I invite her. Tami's recollection is that he invited her to go with me. I think she must have overheard his suggestion. But I do remember inviting her to join us...and that she enthusiastically accepted.

When our day off came, we ate dinner at camp, then left the camp for our date. Doug drove his car with Beki in the passenger seat.

Tami and I sat in the back. We drove to Scout Lake, a small lake about halfway to Sisters.

At camp we operated on standard time instead of daylight savings time, so the evening campfire events would be in the dark. When we arrived at Scout Lake, the sun had already disappeared behind the tall trees. We gathered sticks and built our own campfire. Tami and I sat on one log, and Doug and Beki on another. We all talked and laughed, enjoying each other's company late into the night.

Tami and I began to be drawn together by a mutual chemistry. We enjoyed more days off together that summer. Because the camp's rigorous daily schedule gave us little opportunity to talk to each other, we began writing and passing notes to each other.

It must have become obvious to Gary, the camp director, that Tami and I liked each other. One day he called me to his cabin over the camp intercom. That wasn't unusual. He'd often call me to his cabin to discuss camp business. When I arrived this time, he asked me what I was planning to do for my upcoming day off. He sat at his desk as usual, but with an unusual grin on his face.

"I don't know," I replied.

"Why don't you take your girl for a starlight ride on the three-wheeler to the top of Sand Mountain?" he suggested. "You could take some snacks with you from the camp kitchen."

The Honda ATV was Gary's primary mode of transportation around the camp. He didn't often invite others to use it. He also discouraged his camp staff from dating during the summer–he didn't want the drama to be a distraction.

His offer surprised me. But, I accepted.

It was dark when I started down the camp road in the saddle of the ATV. Tami sat behind me with her arms around my waist. I'd only been to the top of Sand Mountain once before. The path to the mountain was through a maze of dirt roads carved through the forest. I worried a little bit that I'd get us lost.

Sand Mountain is a red, volcanic cinder cone to the west of the the camp. From the camp's waterfront on the eastern shore of Big Lake you can see the rounded top of the mountain rising hundreds of feet above the tree line. A narrow road winds counter-clockwise up the side of the mountain to the rim of its crater. It's all easy to see in the light of day.

That night the brightness of the ATV's headlight blinded me to everything but a short piece of the road ahead of me. I trusted my instincts as I came to forks in the road, and headed in what I thought was the direction of the mountain. When I felt the road suddenly slope upward, I breathed a sigh of relief.

At the summit, I turned off the ATV. Silence replaced the soft growl of the motor. When I turned off the headlight, and our eyes adjusted to the darkness, millions of stars became visible in the sky. Tami and I sat close to each other on the ground. I opened the small paper sack I'd brought with me, and took out two small boxes of raisins, and packages of crackers that I'd brought for our snack. We also each had a small can of apple juice to sip on.

We sat there and talked for a long time, savoring our time together and the amazing view of the stars. I don't remember what we talked about, but the time spent together talking drew us closer together. Tami confessed to me later, she had hoped that I would kiss her right there on the mountain top. I didn't. That first kiss came a few weeks later.

Tami and I continued to make time for each other in the weeks and months ahead. The time spent together, talking, playing and just being with each other drew us closer to each other in our goals and life purpose.

Spending time together can do that when there's a mutual attraction.

Mutual Attraction

There's a mutual attraction between you and God (John 12:32).

God longs to be with you.

God's desire to be with us began with His creation of humanity, and has continued, even in our rebellion against Him.

We see God's desire to be with humanity when He went looking for Adam and Eve in the Garden of Eden, after they sinned. We see it in God reaching out to Abram to be the father of a great nation that would be God's special people. We see it in God asking Moses to set up His tent in the Israelite camp after He rescued them from slavery in Egypt. We see it in Jesus, the Word through which God bound our hearts together with His for eternity.

We use words to build, strengthen, and develop intimacy in relationships.

John 1:1 introduces us to the Word made flesh–Jesus Christ. Jesus came to give us a clearer understanding of God, so that we could draw nearer to Him, and God could draw nearer to us.

Our attraction to God is revealed in our desire to fill our lives with something greater than ourselves, to have meaning and purpose that transcends the fulfillment of our basic needs.

Before Jesus, most people could only catch a glimpse of God through symbolism. But His greatest desire was to have us share an intimate relationship with Him.

After rescuing the Hebrews from slavery in Egypt, God instructed Moses to set up a tabernacle in the wilderness. God specified that a table be set up in what was known as the Holy Place. The Holy Place was the first of two rooms in the tabernacle. God instructed Moses to place 12 loaves of unleavened bread on the golden table. These loaves of flatbread were stacked 6 high to form 2 stacks. A 7-branched, golden candlestick stood across from the table and shone its light on the stacks of bread. The bread represented God the Father and God the Son on their heavenly throne. The candlestick symbolized the Holy Spirit dwelling with God's people and glorifying the Father and Son.

Each Sabbath, the priests were instructed to eat the bread, and place fresh loaves in their place (Leviticus 24:1-9). To eat the bread was a symbol of inviting the enlightened God to live inside of us. There is no greater intimacy than that–to become one with God. Jesus, the Bread of Life (John 6:48-51), prayed for this kind of intimacy:

"I pray that they will all be one, just as you and I are one—as you are in me, Father, and I am in you. And may they be in us so that the world will believe you sent me." John 17:21

Spiritual Intimacy

God's design for a thriving life is one where we are in an intimate relationship with Him. That relationship was broken by sin, but Jesus came to heal it. The process of healing our relationship with God includes entering into an intimate relationship with Him.

While Jesus has returned to sit at the right hand of God, the Holy Spirit dwells with us and in us, if we let Him in. All you have to do is ask.

In the tabernacle, the golden lampstand with 7 branches that stood across from the table of bread was fueled by olive oil, and never allowed to burn out. The light of the lamps illuminated the bread on the table, all day and all night.

The Holy Spirit and the Bible are God with us today. The Bible written by men and inspired by God, illuminated by the Holy Spirit is like Jesus, a fusion of the mortal with the Divine. We can still grow intimate with God by consuming the Bread of Life. His Word–the Bible is our spiritual superfood.

I was hungry. I scooped up some hot lentil soup, and green salad in the market deli. Then I stepped over to the chip aisle to find some nutritious chips to chew on. A broad selection of kale chips in various flavors filled several of the shelves.

If you've never had it, kale is a leafy vegetable, similar to lettuce, but more dense with nutrients and fiber. Kale provides wonderful health benefits. But if you've eaten it, you know it can be a challenge to chew, and not particularly tasty. Eating kale the same way every day would become boring.

Eating the same food the same way every day is boring, no matter how nutritious it is. The joy of eating is lost, even though we need it for survival. This was the experience of the Hebrews in the desert, when God provided them with manna to sustain them on their forty-year journey to the Promised Land. They complained (Numbers 11).

Bible study doesn't have to be boring or tedious.

A Christian without a daily dose of God's Word is spiritually malnourished. No better content for energizing your spiritual life exists than the contents of the Bible. It's impossible to remain a Christian without frequent exposure to the Bible. This is at least the spiritual meaning of Deuteronomy 8:3, as quoted by Jesus when rejecting the tempters enticement to transform stones into bread to satisfy His hunger after fasting 40 days:

"...people do not live by bread alone; rather, we live by every word that comes from the mouth of the LORD."

When we recognize our spiritual malnourishment and hunger, and the spiritual health that we can gain from God's Word, feeding on the Bible becomes less of a chore and more an act of survival. But, its benefits go beyond mere survival-the Bible is spiritual superfood that can sustain a life for eternity.

It empowers us to thrive.

Consider these 4 tips for making Bible study an enjoyable experience.

Before following any of these, always pray to invite the Holy Spirit to illuminate your mind to a full understanding of God's Word.

1. Read

If Bible reading is new to you or you've fought and failed to read from beginning to end, consider taking smaller bites. Put your effort into the quality of your reading rather than the quantity.

Research reveals that reading a printed book offers better retention and understanding for the reader, when compared to an ebook. If you've been reading the Bible on a computer, phone or tablet, and it's just not sinking in, try cracking open a paper copy.

If you've been reading the King James Version (KJV) and getting lost in the unfamiliar vocabulary of seventeenth-century England, try reading from different translations. It can open up new understandings. The much revered and loved KJV has sustained the English-speaking church for centuries. However, just as people whose language is not English benefit from the Bible translated into their own language, those of us who don't speak the Old English of the KJV can benefit from modern English translations.

I like the English Standard Version for its literal approach to translation from the original Hebrew and Greek languages of the Bible. I also like the New Living Translation for its use of conversational English, designed to convey the writer's thoughts rather than exact words.

Read for understanding. Focus on a few verses or a chapter at a time. The Bible promises that in doing this, and in comparing verse to verse, you will gain knowledge and understanding (Isaiah 28:9-10).

When you find a confusing verse, you can compare it to other verses on the same topic using one or more of these tools.

- **Strong's Exhaustive Concordance**, the original Bible study tool, that serves as an index to enable comparison of verses that have the same word, or words. It's available on the web for free and is also available for purchase in print. Just Google it.

- **e-Sword** (http://www.e-sword.net) and **MacSword** (http://macsword.en.softonic.com/mac), free but powerful computer software that automates Strong's Concordance for searching and comparing Bible verses.

- **eSword HD,** an iPhone and iPad Bible study app based on the popular eSword Bible study software for PCs. Find it in the AppStore on your iPhone or iPad.

- **SKJV,** a simple but helpful iPhone and iPad app that automates Strong's Concordance. Find it in the AppStore on your iPhone or iPad.

2. Listen

Faith comes by hearing (Romans 10:17). Hearing the Word can be easily accomplished my reading it out loud.

- Speaker and blogger Keith Ferrin (http://keithferrin.com) provides some useful tips for hearing the Bible. Keith also offers outstanding recitations of books of the Bible.

- Faithcomesbyhearing.com is a non-profit foundation that distributes free audio Bibles around the world, in multiple languages. You may access their free audio Bibles on the web, or by using their free Bible.is iOS and Android apps.

- The You Version Bible app for smartphones and tablets also includes audio versions of the Bible in different translations. A variety of audio Bibles can also be purchased on Amazon.

3. Watch

Word-for-word dramatizations of the Bible can add a new dimension to your understanding of its meaning, as you see the words of the Bible acted out in context. These productions avoid dramatic license that can detract from the text as it reads. Here are the ones I know about:

- *The Gospel of John*
- *The Visual Bible - Matthew*
- *The Visual Bible - Acts*
- *The Jesus Film* is based on the Gospel of Luke, but borrows from other gospels.

Some will take issue with the faithfulness of these productions to the true meaning of the Bible texts on which they are based, and may want to avoid watching these for that reason.

4. Memorize

I find memorization not only allows God to write His Word on my heart, but opens the opportunity for new insights as I continuously repeat a text to engrave it in my mind. While memorization has been done for years using simple methods like flash cards, mobile device apps offer new ways of learning.

Fast.st offers the best flash card system I've seen. You can create and print your own flash cards using their online template or purchase sets from them. The purchased sets come with a vinyl sleeve that makes it easy to carry your memory verses in your pocket or purse.

Here are a couple of easy-to-use memorization apps. Both allow you to easily create your own memory verse lists.

- **RememberMe** available for iOS, Android and the web. It syncs across devices.

- **Scripture Typer** available for iOS, Android and the web. It syncs across devices.

Nourished to Thrive

Feeding on God's Word, you will grow in your understanding of His character, who He is, and His plan for your life. Your goals and purpose will align with God's goals and purpose. The time you spend consuming His Word and in prayer will produce growth in your life like nothing else, infusing you with life for eternity.

Commit yourself to daily Bible reading and memorization as part of your morning routine. Start each day with nourished with spiritual superfood by consuming God's Word.

Habit 5 - Give God's Grace: How to Overcome Selfishness and Love People More

Love is patient and kind. Love is not jealous or boastful or proud or rude. It does not demand its own way. It is not irritable, and it keeps no record of being wronged. It does not rejoice about injustice but rejoices whenever the truth wins out. Love never gives up, never loses faith, is always hopeful, and endures through every circumstance.

1 Corinthians 13:4-7

Our marriage hit the rocks on our honeymoon.

We'd chosen Tami's dad to perform our wedding ceremony. One of Dick's conditions in marrying us was that we participate in pre-marital counseling. He arranged for us to receive counseling from a colleague, Pastor Chad McComas nearby in Corvallis, Oregon.

To prepare for our counseling sessions, Pastor Chad had us take the Meyers-Briggs personality inventory. The results highlighted something we knew intuitively—our personality types were at polar opposites of each other. Tami was an extrovert, I was an introvert. I was intuitive, Tami was sensing. Tami was thinking, I was feeling. I was perceiving, Tami judging.

Tami and I thought of ourselves as being complimentary, but Pastor Chad warned that our personality differences could also become a source of conflict in our marriage. In so many words, he asked if we were sure we wanted to get married.

It was too late to turn back. We couldn't imagine being happy without each other.

A Perfect Wedding...Almost

I'd asked Tami to marry me on Christmas Eve. We'd had about 5 months to plan our wedding. The date was set for the Sunday of Memorial Day weekend. Tami and I went over every detail of the wedding together: colors, clothing, flowers, music, reception and vows.

I'd planned the honeymoon myself. But Tami insisted I let her in on the plans. She was relentless in her persistence. I finally gave in.

We didn't have much money. We had a small budget for our honeymoon. I'd be graduating from college the weekend after our wedding. I'd been a full-time student with a few jobs on campus. Tami worked part-time for a doctor's office. I'd planned a simple getaway to a hotel on the Oregon coast. Tami wanted something a little more romantic. So, we cancelled the hotel and planned on five days at the Inn at Otter Crest, an oceanfront resort.

After the honeymoon, and my graduation, we planned to spend one more summer at Big Lake Youth Camp. After camp, I'd start my job as an assistant boys' dean in a co-ed boarding school in southern Oregon. Tami had been promised a job managing housekeeping in the girls' dormitory. I was told we'd be assigned a small two-bedroom house on the campus, near the boys' dorm.

While our jobs were lined up, we hadn't given much thought to what married life would be like. We assumed it would be great. But Tami and I had no clue what those first weeks, months and years would be like.

Our wedding at her dad's church in Albany, Oregon, was almost perfect. Tami was beautiful in her white wedding gown. The church was full of family and friends. I was nervous but happier than I'd ever been. I even shed some tears of joy. But I had no clue that within a few days my happiness would be shattered.

After the wedding, Tami and I mingled with our guests at the reception. I'm not one that enjoys small talk. It didn't take me long to thank people for coming, and to say hello to people I hadn't seen in a while. We had about a 90-minute drive ahead of us. I was looking forward to starting our honeymoon.

A Sour Honeymoon

After running through the customary shower of rice thrown at us by our guests, we climbed into my brown Mazda GLC and drove the short distance to Tami's parents' home. Someone had painted "Just Married" on the rear window. Strings of aluminum pop cans tied to my rear bumper clanked as they bounced on the road. At my in-laws', we changed out of our wedding clothes into clothes that were more comfortable, grabbed our travel bags, untied the strings of pop cans, and hit the road for our honeymoon destination.

It was only the second day of our honeymoon, Tami announced she was homesick. She wanted to end our honeymoon early. She wanted us to go home to her parents. She missed them.

I had an unexpected reaction. I felt emotions flare up inside me. My chest tightened. I felt fear. I felt anger. I wanted to scream. I wanted to run. I felt hot. I felt like I could explode. I'd never felt this way before.

Tami's announcement shocked me. From the time we'd made our vows to each other, I'd thought our marriage was off to a good start. But suddenly, it seemed to me that she didn't love me as much as I thought. I tried to make sense of what she was saying, but it seemed crazy to me. After we said "I do" we were supposed to live happily ever after. Now, it seemed she wasn't happy. I thought I was all she needed, but now it seemed I wasn't enough.

I over-reacted. I see that now. Back then, I was full of insecurities. My sense of who I was and my purpose in life was vague. My identity was wrapped up in being happily married, and now it seemed that I wasn't. I'd kept my insecure self thinly veiled. Sensing a threat, my negative emotions rushed to the front line in my defense.

I accused Tami of not loving me. I called her crazy. Just days before, I'd vowed to love Tami for the rest of our lives together. But at that moment, I was more interested in myself than in how she felt. I left her in our room alone, and went for a walk.

Which Wolf Do You Feed?

The story is told of a wise Cherokee brave who sat quietly at the side of his grandson one fall evening. The grandfather and the boy warmed themselves in the glow of a small campfire. Perhaps the older man had noticed a spark in his grandson that a wind might stir into an uncontrolled blaze.

"There is a battle fought inside the heart of each man," the grandfather said. "It is a battle between two wolves.

"One wolf is evil. It is filled with hatred, envy, greed, impatience, deception, despair, fear and rage.

"The other wolf is good. It is filled with love, gratitude, generosity, peace, joy, honesty, patience, hope, and kindness."

The grandfather paused and waited.

The grandson locked his gaze on the fire. The grandfather watched out of the corner of his eye. He could see the boy thinking. The silence was broken only by the crackle of burning wood.

When the right amount of time had passed, the grandson turned his eyes toward his grandfather's and asked, "Which wolf wins?"

Their eyes still connected, the grandfather offered this simple answer: "The one that you feed."

I'd been feeding the evil wolf for a long time, and didn't know it. I'd been feeding the good wolf, too. But I'd been keeping the evil wolf alive enough, that when the opportunity came, it pounced on the good wolf, and lashed out with its fierce fangs to bite into Tami.

Growing Bitterness

I agreed to end our honeymoon a day early. We spent an awkward day at the in-laws'. Then we drove to Walla Walla University for my graduation weekend. After my graduation, we returned to the in-laws' for a couple of weeks, until it was time for us to report to staff orientation at camp.

Since our honeymoon, I'd felt a numbness. In the days before our wedding, I'd expected to feel extremely happy afterward. My happiness lasted a little more than 24 hours. My disappointment wasn't just in Tami's homesickness. The passion we had for being with each other that we felt before the wedding evaporated during our honeymoon. Rather than feeling bonded to each other by love, I felt stuck to someone who didn't seem happy to be with me.

The opposing personality traits that Pastor Chad warned us about began to push us away from each other.

Over the weeks and months ahead, I became bitter. I'd keep it inside, until Tami did something else that disappointed me. I'd see it as a threat. Then I'd lash out at her with angry, hurtful words.

Are You Surviving or Thriving?

The neurons of your brain form pathways through which information travels, and impulses stimulate actions. The more often these pathways get used, the more habitual our responses become to certain types of experiences.

Our ancestors, like us, struggled to survive in a sin-stained world. Hundreds of years ago, survival was more difficult than it is for those of us who have access to grocery stores, public safety services, and modern healthcare. Their survival depended on protecting themselves and their families from starvation, danger and early death by banding together in tribes for farming, foraging and hunting. Tribes also offered strength to defend against enemy attacks. The behaviors of our ancestors produced instinctive behaviors that were passed on to their descendants. As a result, you and I have inherited neural pathways intended to help us survive and defend ourselves against starvation and danger.

When the pie is cut for dessert, I look for the biggest piece. Sometimes I don't let the car next to me merge into my lane. I've imagined myself launching attacks against rude neighbors.

Survival instinct tells me to grab the biggest piece of pie, in case there's no food tomorrow. I don't want to let the car next to me merge, because I "need" to get to the "kill" before there's nothing left for me to eat. I want to take down my neighbor to protect myself and my family from future threats.

Most of those inherited pathways are negative. Negative pathways make us prone to respond to experiences with behaviors better suited for survival than for thriving.

Survival begins with instincts encoded in what scientists refer to as the primitive part of our brain. Instincts are the things we do without having to think about doing them.

But survival is about having enough to assure safety, endure cold and prevent hunger. If we feed our survival instinct by repeatedly surrendering to it, we reap selfishness. Thriving is about overcoming fear with kindness, and having an abundance that can be shared. To cultivate kindness and generosity we need to repeatedly surrender to God's influence in our lives.

Three years into our marriage, Tami and I hit a wall. She refused to put up with my selfish actions. She insisted we get marriage counseling. I resisted at first. It was a pride thing. I was a trained counselor. I helped people overcome their problems, but was ashamed to admit I had problems of my own. But realizing the alternative was divorce, I surrendered to God's influence and reluctantly embraced humility. I wouldn't allow myself to fall any farther. I agreed to ask for help.

We found a Christian psychologist who helped us turn things around. He helped me see that while my selfish behavior might guarantee my survival, it was keeping me from thriving in my faith, my relationship with Tami, and my work.

It took several weeks to turn our marriage around, and months to heal the open wounds in our relationship.

I'm not as selfish as I used to be. But I haven't overcome all my selfish habits and replaced them with selfless ones.

You're probably in a similar position.

Perhaps you wish you could say you're a selfless, self-sacrificing person. You want to love the way that God loves. You want grace—to love for love's sake, not because it's earned or deserved. You want a thriving love that has the strength of an old oak tree, whose leaf-laden branches provide comforting shade for everything around it, just because it can. You want 1 Corinthians 13 kind of love. But the virtues of love in that passage of Scripture don't describe you very well.

Where Love Thrives

Thriving begins in the frontal lobe of our brain. It's the part of the brain where we reason, use judgment, make decisions, and exercise self-control.

Human love requires reasoning that can only occur in the frontal lobe of the brain. Love is not a basic survival instinct. Sexual desire is. But taken to its extreme, love will lead a person to choose self-sacrifice for the survival of others. Sexual lust won't.

The basic survival instincts make it more likely that we will produce the next generation of humans, so that our tribe will survive. Survival instinct ensures that there will be children, and that they will be kept safe, warm and fed.

Human love ensures that those children will have a nurturing mother and father, and a caring community of people committed to helping them become the best they can be. Where instinct makes it possible for humans to survive into the next generation, love makes it possible for humans to thrive.

But we must feed the love.

You've probably heard the phrase "Knowledge is power."

There's something more powerful–Love.

God is love. There's nothing more powerful than God.

For love to transcend our survival instincts, we must carve new pathways in our brain by developing new habits. New habits take root and last longer when they're cultivated by the power of God's love stimulating our frontal lobe.

The Habits of Thriving Love

Here are 7 habits I'm asking God cultivate in my life to allow the selfless, self-sacrificing love of God to flourish in me and overflow to others. I recommend these habits to you:

1. Choose love.

Make a conscious choice every day to love. As you start your day, receive God's love with gratitude. Invite God to cultivate His kind of love in your heart.

Thank God for loving you enough to allow His Son Jesus to suffer and die for your sin. Thank God for reaching out across the universe to rescue you from being lost forever, and to bring you home to live with Him for eternity. And savor the simple blessings you receive each day, like air to breathe, clean water to drink, and food to eat.

2. Welcome love.

When we're expecting guests in our home, we spend extra time cleaning. We want to give our guests a warm welcome. We want to show them respect. That's one way we show we care about them.

When we choose love, we're inviting God to send His Spirit as a guest into our lives. The apostle Paul said our body is a temple for the Holy Spirit (1 Corinthians 6:19). The Bible records God's instructions for the care of our body temple, including what to think about, what to listen to, what to watch, and how to eat. Following these instructions equips our brain to work better, making it easier to manage our thoughts and emotions so we can love more.

3. Contemplate love.

Spend time each day observing perfect love in action. Read the Bible and witness the amazing love of God for humanity. The greatest expression of God's love is revealed in the Gospels of Matthew, Mark, Luke and John.

My favorite gospel is John, because it reads like a love story. But evidence of God's love can be discovered on every page of the Bible. Look for it, find it, dwell on it.

4. Practice humility.

Choose the smallest piece of pie. Give someone your seat. Apologize for your mistakes. Forgive people who wrong you. Do work that is "below your pay grade."

Pride is the greatest barrier to receiving and giving love. We tell ourselves we don't need love. We convince ourselves others don't deserve our love.

We need to receive the mind of Jesus Christ, who acted as if others were more important than He is (Philippians 2:2-7). To receive the mind of Christ, we need to stop resisting it. We resist the mind of Christ by persisting as if our way is the most important way.

5. Practice kindness.

Compliment your spouse and your children. Pick up someone else's dropped item and return it to them. Allow the car alongside you to merge into your lane. Greet your rude neighbor with a smile.

Kindness softens our heart toward others. The King James Version of the Bible uses the word "gentleness" instead of "kindness" when describing the fruit of the Spirit (Galatians 5:22).

6. Practice patience.

Patience requires that we accept that some things are out of our control. Patience also requires that we not try to control others. And patience sometimes requires us to wait and allow things to move at their own pace.

To accept something is to acknowledge that it is what it is. It's like gravity-no matter how much you want to change it, it's going to be there as much as it was before you tried to change it.

Accept that your family isn't going to be ready for church at the same speed as you. Accept that you and others will not learn at the expected pace, and will forget stuff and make mistakes. Accept that the traffic will move at the same speed, no matter how much you honk the car horn or ride the tail of the car ahead of you.

7. Give generously.

Give someone else the last piece of pie. Pay for your coworker's lunch. Buy that one thing your spouse has been wanting, instead of that new gadget you've been dreaming about.

It's been said that true generosity is measured not by how much we give, but by how much we have left over.

Feed the Love

Which of these actions are already habits for you? Which of these actions do you want to make a habit? Choose at least one and start practicing it today. Practice until you do it without thinking about it. Feed it, cultivate it, and live to thrive.

Habit 6 - Defend God's People: How to Overcome Evil with Good

Don't be selfish; don't try to impress others. Be humble, thinking of others as better than yourselves. Don't look out only for your own interests, but take an interest in others, too. You must have the same attitude that Christ Jesus had.

Philippians 2:3-5

Whenever evil causes pain and suffering in any part of the world, it threatens all of us.

My neighbor Bill served as an altar boy in his youth. Like too many altar boys entrusted to the care of Roman Catholic priests, Bill suffered sexual abuse from his priest. As an adult, Bill and others who'd been molested by this priest have sought what justice could still be attained.

Some have sought justice for their own benefit. We all have a survival instinct that drives us to eliminate all threats to our safety. Taken to the extreme, it drives us to revenge that is only satisfied when the one who hurt us feels pain, and dies for their sin.

Some have sought justice to make the world a safer place, not only for themselves, but for as many as possible. Taken to the extreme, Jesus felt the pain and died for the sin of the most unworthy sinner, so that if he or she chose, they could step out of the darkness, and become channels of light into the world.

My neighbor Bill sought to make the world a safer place by pursuing justice through the courts, but not for personal gain. He took an extra step. As a memorial to the brokenness he and others suffered, Bill commissioned a millstone memorial to be chiseled from granite. He put it on display in the entry of a church in our neighborhood. At Bill's invitation, I went to see it.

Bill and I, and a few others in the room, stood around the millstone in silence, contemplating Jesus' solemn warning engraved in the granite:

> "But if you cause one of these little ones who trusts in me to fall into sin, it would be better for you to be thrown into the sea with a large millstone hung around your neck." Mark 9:42

Jesus' words are a promise that God is the ultimate arbiter of justice. God's justice is fair, and not fueled by hatred for those who've done us wrong. Knowing that we can trust the final outcome to God, we can put our hatred aside and know that God will hand down the appropriate sentence to those who've chosen evil instead of good.

In Charleston, South Carolina, 13 people gathered for a Bible study at Emanuel African Methodist Episcopal Church. One of those was Dylann Roof, a young man unknown to the others in the room. The rest of those gathered gave the stranger a warm welcome. Later, as others in the meeting began praying, someone saw Roof slip a handgun from his fanny pack. A witness says Roof pointed the gun at 87-year-old Susie Jackson. After an unsuccessful attempt to persuade Roof to put the gun away, Ms. Jackson's grand-nephew Tywanza Sanders put himself between Roof and Ms. Jackson. He took the first bullet and his last breath to save her life. But Ms. Jackson and 7 others also died from gunshot wounds that night.

Roof was arrested the next day. A day later, at a bond hearing in a Charleston County courtroom, relatives of the dead, and survivors of the shooting, took turns speaking to Roof in front of the court. In an unusual act of grace, each one offered their forgiveness to Roof.

The Root of Evil

The negative emotions of distrust, envy and fear are often the seeds from which evil sprouts. When evil takes root in a person, and is cultivated by feeding negative emotions, it spreads and brings pain and suffering to that person, and to those around him or her. The effect of one person's evil can ripple through a family, and community, bearing fruit of unspeakable violence against parents and children, at home, school, church or the public mall. As we've seen in the atrocities committed under the leadership of evil men like Adolf Hitler, and Osama Bin Laden, evil influence can spread through an entire nation, and around the world.

Among the greatest evils is when a person threatens a family. Words and actions designed to hurt, control or steal from a spouse, parent or child, tear down the ability of their victims to love and trust others.

Where love builds bridges to bring people together, evil tears down those bridges and creates deep chasms that break up marriages, families, communities, churches, and countries.

When I reacted to my wife's homesickness on our honeymoon with hurtful words, fear and distrust planted a seed that I cultivated by feeding those negative emotions. Evil took root in my heart and created a chasm between me and Tami. Over time, my words and actions deepened and widened that chasm to the point we were more like roommates than lovers.

When Adam and Eve distrusted God, and ate the forbidden fruit, a seed of evil was planted in this world. By the time their son Cain murdered his brother Abel out of envy, evil had taken root. In only 10 generations, from Adam to Noah, evil had so infected and flourished in humanity, God chose to start over.

When Noah and his family stepped out of the ark after the Great Flood into a world cleansed of all that had gone wrong with it before, they had every opportunity to live right. But, Ham couldn't resist his natural tendencies toward evil, and in disrespect for his father Noah, he invited a curse upon his descendants.

Since the fall of humanity's parents in Eden, it's been the natural tendency of people to look out for their own interests at the expense of others. But the "survival of the fittest" instinct is only good for keeping us safe, fed and clothed, and for producing the next generation of children. Relying on our survival instinct as a way of life doesn't enable us to thrive.

When allowed to rule our lives, the survival instinct produces in us what the Bible calls the "works of the flesh":

> "When you follow the desires of your sinful nature, the results are very clear: sexual immorality, impurity, lustful pleasures, idolatry, sorcery, hostility, quarreling, jealousy, outbursts of anger, selfish ambition, dissension, division,

envy, drunkenness, wild parties, and other sins like these. Let me tell you again, as I have before, that anyone living that sort of life will not inherit the Kingdom of God." Galatians 5:19-21

Bearing Good Fruit

When we allow the Holy Spirit to cultivate God's character in our lives, the higher powers of our brain are activated and empowered to produce the "fruits of the Spirit":

"But the Holy Spirit produces this kind of fruit in our lives: love, joy, peace, patience, kindness, goodness, faithfulness, gentleness, and self-control. There is no law against these things!" Galatians 5:22-23

The difference between surviving and thriving is the survival instinct turns our focus inward, in service to our selfish desire. The thriving life is one that enables us to look out for the needs and interests of others with at least the same level of concern we have for our own needs and interests.

That's what Jesus did. And through the influence of Jesus' goodness, individuals, families, communities, and nations have been changed for the better. God calls you and me to have the same kind of influence.

It's a call to defend God's people, approaching them with a forgiving heart, and offering our help to rescue them whatever evil has come upon them.

> "Don't be selfish; don't try to impress others. Be humble, thinking of others as better than yourselves. Don't look out only for your own interests, but take an interest in others, too. You must have the same attitude that Christ Jesus had." Philippians 2:3-5

We might find it easy to defend people we like. But how do you defend someone who has taken the life of someone you loved and offer them forgiveness? I don't believe it just happens. It's the result of answering God's call to receive a thriving faith, surrendering to the influence of the Holy Spirit, and cultivated by meditating on the life and words of Jesus, and through daily prayer and meditation.

When we answer God's call, receive the Holy Spirit, pray and meditate on His Word, His character begins to rub off on us.

Defending the Defenseless

God's character transformation includes producing within us a passion to defend the defenseless.

Just as Jesus was sent to be our Defender, God sends Christians out into the world to defend the oppressed, the poor, the widows, the homeless, the naked, the hungry and the orphans (Isaiah 19:20; James 1:27).

The early Christian church put much effort and resources into making sure every person in their community received love in a tangible way. They also extended love to those outside their community.

Love can't be just talk. The gospel of Jesus is as much about action as it is about words.

The gospel without works is dead.

Good works are as much about how I take care of others, as they are about how I take care of me.

The second greatest commandment is to love your neighbor as yourself (Matthew 19:19). The apostle Paul put it this way:

"Don't look out for only your own interests, but also look out for the interests of others." Philippians 2:4

The Old Testament prophet Isaiah can be called "the gospel prophet." More than any other Old Testament prophet, he saw the coming Messiah.

Isaiah's prophetic book provided a part of Jesus' road map during His life on earth. So, it ought to provide a road map for us–if we want to be like Jesus.

One of the passages from this book that motivates me to draw closer to God is Isaiah 58:6-11. It motivates me to draw closer to God, because I need the power of God to turn these words into action in my life.

The passage comes with a call to defend the defenseless, and it promises happiness and healing to those who answer the call.

As God's messenger, Isaiah calls each of us to do these 7 things:

1. Untie people from the bonds of sin.
2. Free people from oppression.
3. Give food and the word of life to those who hunger.
4. Provide shelter to the homeless.
5. Provide clothing to the naked.

6. Don't accuse others.

7. Don't speak false words.

Here's what God promises to do when we answer this call:

1. God will answer your prayers.

2. God will heal you quickly.

3. God will make your light shine in the darkness.

4. God will guide you continually.

5. God will quench your unfulfilled desires.

6. God will strengthen your bones.

7. God will cause you to thrive like a watered garden, and everlasting spring.

This sounds good to me. How about you? What evil threatens to draw you or your loved ones into a dark place today? Choose to shine a light on it by overcoming evil with good.

Habit 7 - Glorify God's Name: Doing What You're Called to Do

He is the stone that makes people stumble, the rock that makes them fall. They stumble because they do not obey God's word, and so they meet the fate that was planned for them. But you are not like that, for you are a chosen people. You are royal priests, a holy nation, God's very own possession. As a result, you can show others the goodness of God, for he called you out of the darkness into his wonderful light.

1 Peter 2:8-9

Walking through life without doing what God has called you to do is like sentencing a flourishing, flowering plant to live in complete darkness. The life of the plant withers. There's no growth, just a slow, meaningless death.

When I was 12 years old, Dad took me and my brother Tyler from our home in Jacksonville, Oregon, on a short road trip to Oregon

Caves National Monument. The caves provide a unique opportunity to step into the underworld of stalactites and stalagmites.

Cave exploring, known as spelunking among the sport's enthusiasts, attracts a unique type of adventurer. As a sport, spelunking provides a different kind of thrill than that experienced by scaling the side of a rock, summiting a mountain peak, or finishing first in an endurance race. Avid spelunkers are explorers. They relish the possibility that they are the first humans to step– or crawl–through an underground tunnel, or discover a hidden chamber, sealed off from the rest of us by layers of rock and veils of darkness.

This was my first spelunking adventure. It didn't provide all the thrill that pumps up dedicated spelunkers. It did allow me to sample a bit of what excites them. As our tour started, we stepped below the earth's relatively warm surface, leaving the streams of light that filtered through the evergreen trees that surrounded the cave's entrance. We ventured with our tour group into the cave's mouth where the temperature quickly dropped to 44 degrees Fahrenheit. Electric light bulbs strung out on cables overhead lit the way for us to navigate the narrow paths and stair steps carved between rocky crevasses, down into an underworld of fascinating marble formations created by the natural flow of water against rock.

Into the Darkness

Stopping in a cavern deep inside the cave, our guide asked us to turn off our flashlights, if we had one. Then, he flipped a switch, cutting the power to the lights overhead. I could almost feel the darkness envelop me, as I stood there with my eyes open and saw nothing but blackness.

Curious about what a little light would do, I turned on the tiny light in my digital wristwatch. Its faint glow illuminated the outline of my hand above it.

No matter how thick the darkness, the glow of a little light will pierce it.

About eight years later, while working on the staff at Big Lake Youth Camp in the Central Oregon Cascade Mountains, I joined a group of camp counselors in training on a spelunking expedition. The caves we explored didn't compare in size or beauty to the Oregon Caves. These were lava tubes.

One cave started as a black hole in the ground about 4 feet wide. We lowered ourselves into the hole with our flashlights in hand into a small room. As we trekked deeper into the cave, at times we got on our hands and knees to crawl through tunnels narrow enough that there was no turning back. If we panicked, the only way out was crawling backwards–no turning around.

I gripped my flashlight, and did what I could to keep my imagination under control as I pictured walls caving in and trapping us.

The absence of light in these caves meant nothing grew there, except deposits of lime and minerals washed from the rock above by water. That's how the stalactites and stalagmites form. And for spelunkers, a flashlight is a lifeline. If you're deep in the cave without a light to show you the way out, you're lost.

Light in Dark Times

In the period known in history as the Dark Ages, possession of a Bible was a punishable crime. A corrupt church, sharing the same bed with equally corrupt governments, relentlessly persecuted Christians who had chosen as their life purpose to sow God's Word like seeds wherever they could.

Among these faithful missionaries, the people known as Waldenses were the most enduring. For hundreds of years they made the mountains of northern Italy their fortress. They would venture into lowland villages to engage in commerce and trade only for the purpose of finding fertile hearts in which to plant handwritten transcripts of the Bible, or to whom they could speak words of hope.

The Waldenses shined their little lights in faithfulness to Jesus' Great Commission (Matthew 28:16-20). They pursued this path in spite of retaliation, withstanding ruthless massacre and torment for opposing the Roman papacy and its puppet kings. But their little lights kindled the flames of the Protestant Reformation, enabling God's Word to dispel the religious and political corruption that had darkened Europe, and freeing multitudes from the oppression of physical and spiritual bondage.

The world still needs light. Darkness still binds people to corrupt governments and spiritual confusion. Without even a little light to show them the way out, they'll die. They can't grow. They'll be lost. Many will die a meaningless death, locked in darkness.

The Light of God's Character

God is the main character in all of the Bible. From Genesis to Revelation, the Bible reveals His character. The purpose of the Bible, and the reason it's recorded for us, is that we may see God's character, and be drawn to Him.

God's character draws us like a bright light that dispels darkness.

> "This is the message we heard from Jesus and now declare to you: God is light, and there is no darkness in him at all." 1 John 1:5

Jesus said:

> "I am the light of the world. If you follow me, you won't have to walk in darkness, because you will have the light that leads to life." John 8:12

Most mornings I walk on a path around the pasture on our 5-acre farm where we raise Boer goats and care for honeybees. On clear mornings I can see the hills on the eastern horizon. Beyond those hills, Mt. Hood's peak sits above the horizon, white with snow. But until the sun rises, it sits in darkness. As the sun starts a new day, an orange glow grows behind the shaded silhouette of the mountain, and eventually bursts into a bright display of sunlight across the hills and over the pasture.

Seeing the sunrise this way is worth savoring. There's a certain amount of glory to it.

The light of God's character is His glory.

While Moses and the Hebrews camped in the Sinai desert on their way to the Promised Land, Moses asked to see God's glory. God directed Moses to stand in the crevice of a rock. Shielding Moses from the light of His glory with His hand as He passed, God let Moses see His back side. And as God passed, He declared His glory:

> The LORD passed in front of Moses, calling out, "Yahweh! The LORD! The God of compassion and mercy! I am slow to anger and filled with unfailing love and faithfulness. I lavish unfailing love to a thousand generations. I forgive iniquity, rebellion, and sin. But I do not excuse the guilty. I lay the sins of the parents upon their children and grandchildren; the entire family is affected— even children in the third and fourth generations." Exodus 34:6-7

God's glory gives light to those who dwell in His presence. When Jesus revealed to John a vision of the New Jerusalem, John described it that way:

> "And the city has no need of sun or moon, for the glory of God illuminates the city, and the Lamb [Jesus, the Son of God] is its light." Revelation 21:23

Out of the Darkness

God created Adam and Eve with a perfect character. They were covered with robes of God's light–His glory. Their sin in eating the forbidden fruit wasn't the result of a flaw in their character, but an informed choice. God had warned them of the consequences of their choice: Death. But they chose to believe the lie that has been repeated throughout human history: You can be like God without following His instructions, and live. God's glory left them, and they saw they were naked.

We've all believed the lie at least once in our lives. At best, we end up complacent, coasting through life as if nothing matters but the pleasure we can achieve in the moment. But complacency eventually leads to death. God's glory leaves us, and without it we have no life-giving power to sustain us.

In drawing us to Himself, God invites us to align our lives with the truth, to have His glory cover us, and to be sustained and flourish in His life-giving power. The truth is that we can be like God, but only by following His instructions. God wants to recreate His character in us. When He does, our lives will give glory to God's name.

Jesus said it this way:

"You are the light of the world—like a city on a hilltop that cannot be hidden. No one lights a lamp and then puts it under a basket. Instead, a lamp is placed on a stand, where it gives light to everyone in the house. In the same way, let your good deeds shine out for all to see, so that everyone will praise your heavenly Father." Matthew 5:14-16

Receiving the Light

God created us to operate best within certain parameters. When we live within those parameters, we grow and we thrive in our faith, relationships and work. When we step outside those parameters, it's like putting a flourishing, flowering plant in darkness—we stop growing and start dying.

Each habit I've encouraged you to develop up to this point is intended to align you with God's instructions, to cultivate growth, so you can overcome the hopelessness and complacency that lead to death, and live to thrive. When you live to thrive, light will shine through you not just for your own benefit, but also for the benefit of others.

Every one of us is surrounded by an atmosphere of light or darkness. An atmosphere of light emits faith, courage, hope and love. An atmosphere of darkness spreads the gloom of discontent, selfishness, and apathy. Whatever our atmosphere, it consciously and unconsciously affects everyone around us.

The habits of thriving faith, relationships and work produce a positive atmosphere. But none of these habits stands on its own with the same kind of strength of character they produce together. One habit alone is like a one-key piano. It can produce one note. Put all the habits together, and you have an instrument that can play an attractive tune. But the tune is incomplete without this last note–giving glory to God's name.

If you've applied the previously presented habits to your life, then you've been cultivating a lifestyle that reflects God's character.

- God is love.
- God is grateful.
- God is healing.
- God is truthful.
- God is generous.
- God defends the defenseless.

How to Give Light to Our World (GLOW)

This seventh habit gives us the ultimate purpose for practicing the first six: to give glory to God by giving light to our world. God's glory is His character, and by cultivating the growth of His character in us, we become channels of God's light to the world, dispelling any darkness around us with the glow of a thriving life.

This is God's calling.

> "Always be joyful. Never stop praying. Be thankful in all circumstances, for this is God's will for you who belong to Christ Jesus. Do not stifle the Holy Spirit. Do not scoff at prophecies, but test everything that is said. Hold on to what is good. Stay away from every kind of evil. Now may the God of peace make you holy in every way, and may your whole spirit and soul and body be kept blameless until our Lord Jesus Christ comes again. God will make this happen, for he who calls you is faithful." 1 Thessalonians 5:16-24

Your calling is what you were meant to do-your ultimate purpose.

Some have lost hope of a purpose. Others could care less about having a purpose. Many people wander in circles, wondering what that ultimate purpose is-confused and looking for clarity in finding their calling.

My high school yearbook lists my future profession as "Graphic Designer." As I mentioned in Chapter 2, I enrolled in college in a major called "Recreation"

Near the end of my freshman year, my advisor called me into his office. Coach Windemuth broke it to me gently. The university was dropping the recreation major. On the coach's advice, I changed my major to physical education.

After my sophomore year, I took a year off from my studies to work in youth ministry. After that, I decided to change my major to social work. That's the major I graduated with.

After graduation, I started a job as an assistant boys' dean at a boarding high school. I took the job thinking it was my calling.

I didn't fully understand what I was trying to do, but as I look back, I can see that I was looking for a way to give light to the world.

About half way through the school year the principal called me into his office. It was the day after I lost my temper with one of my students. The boy had stolen the head dean's chocolate birthday cake while we waited for him to arrive for a surprise party. When I discovered the theft, I charged in to the boy's dormitory room where he and a few of his buddies were eating the cake, and I called the boy a name I won't repeat here.

By the end of the school year I realized that being a dormitory dean wasn't for me. I applied for jobs managing retirement homes, and applied to graduate school. By the time summer arrived, I decided to return to school for a master of social work degree.

After earning my master's, I took a job as a substance abuse counselor. A few years later I went to work at a mental health clinic. After that I took a job in customer service in a health insurance company.

I've gone through a few career changes since then.

Through all of these changes, this thought lingered in the back of my mind: "Is this all there is?" In moments of despair, it made it to the forefront.

I was challenged by the question, "Why am I here?"

I was looking for my calling.

Some people find a calling that lasts a lifetime. Some might live out their lives as missionaries in a third-world country, bringing hope to the hopeless. Others may serve as entrepreneurs, starting businesses that fill a need in their community. Or healthcare professionals, bringing healing to hurting people.

Others have callings that change with the seasons of life. They may start their career in a corporate cubicle, and work their way up to a corner office, and later start their own business. Some may serve as a pastor, and later a counselor or an attorney. Some may start their career as an administrative assistant, later decide to stay home to raise their kids, then volunteer for a charitable organization after the kids grow up.

Whether their calling is a life-long adventure, or a series of unrelated adventures, all of these people will have one thing in common: If their calling is from God, they'll be giving light to the world and giving glory to God's name.

I've arrived at the conclusion that I'm in the category of people that has a new calling for each season of life.

I've also realized that my calling transcends my career and what my job might be at any particular time. Underlying whatever work I take on, my calling is a way of life.

Consider this: Your calling may not be the work that you do, but the way you do your work. There's a difference. If your calling is the work you do, your purpose in life could begin and end with your current job. If your calling is a state of mind that affects how you do your work, your purpose in life stays with you, regardless of the work that's in front of you. You could even do what you're called to do without a job. When your calling is the way you do your work, it can be the way you live your life–the way you listen to, talk to, and touch the people around you.

Your calling can be a lifestyle–a lifestyle of thriving in faith, relationships and work, that spreads light wherever you are.

To turn the 6 habits that come before this one into a lifestyle, take these 4 steps. Following these steps changes the way I practice my faith, engage in relationships, and do my work. It could do the same for you. It could be the difference between living a life that's growing in the light and giving light to others, or dying a meaningless death in darkness.

1. Trust in God's Guidance

I'm learning to see God leading in my life. As I look back in my life to the point where I chose to follow Jesus, I see how God has prepared me for what I'm doing today. I trust that God's also preparing me for work He has lined up for me tomorrow.

I keep in mind that God often uses difficult experiences in life to polish us, so that the reflection of His light on us shines brighter than it did before. The challenges may come from any direction, impacting every aspect of who we are. The trials that polish us may burnish our faith, our relationships, our work, or even our health, like a potter adding glaze to a clay pot. Trusting in God during these times makes it possible for me to grow and glow brighter.

> "Trust in the LORD with all your heart; do not depend on your own understanding. Seek his will in all you do, and he will show you which path to take." Proverbs 3:5-6

2. Learn to Recognize God's Voice

Reading the Bible, and putting its words to memory, I grow in my ability to recognize God's voice.

When my wife Tami and I were dating each other before we married, we wrote love letters to each other. When I got a letter from Tami, I'd hear her voice in my mind as I read the words on each page. It was almost as if she was in the room talking to me.

God's Word expressed in the Bible is a reflection of His voice. As I read the words He spoke to the Old Testament prophets I become acquainted with His voice. Reading Jesus' words recorded in the New Testament, I hear Him speaking to me.

> "So faith comes from hearing, and hearing through the word of God." Romans 10:17 NKJV

3. Listen for God's Voice

I'm learning to keep my mind open to God's voice. He speaks to me first through the Bible (2 Timothy 3:16-17). But I also hear God's voice in nature, music, impressions, my conscience, and the counsel of other believers.

My stubbornness can lead me to ignore God's voice. So, I cultivate an attitude of humility by choosing to surrender my will to God's wisdom. The noise and demands of the day can drown out God's voice. So, I make room for quiet time each morning where God and I can be alone without interruption, and draw closer to each other.

> "And your ears shall hear a word behind you, saying, 'This is the way, walk in it," when you turn to the right or when you turn to the left.'" Isaiah 30:21 ESV

4. Commit to Glorifying God

When Moses met with God on Mt. Sinai, God's glory left a glow on Moses' face.

When Jesus tells us to let our light shine, it's a call to spend time with God, let His character rub off on us, and to reflect God's character in our life (Matthew 5:16).

God's character is revealed by the fruit of the Spirit in our words and actions: Love, joy, peace, patience, kindness, goodness, faithfulness, gentleness, and self-control (Galatians 5:22-23).

Allow God to cultivate this fruit in your life.

I'm learning in tending to my small orchard of fruits trees, berries and grapes, that the quality of the fruit is directly tied to the nutrition and care of the plant. While there are other factors involved, like weather and pests, the health of a plant can be the difference between surviving drought and pests, and losing a crop of fruit.

To cultivate the fruit of the Spirit in our lives, we first invite God to be the gardener. Then we accept the nourishment He provides in the Bible, through fellowship with other followers of Jesus, and through communion with Him in prayer and meditation. And we submit to His pruning, as He removes the things from our lives that will pull nutrients away from our fruit and block light from entering our hearts.

> "So whether you eat or drink, or whatever you do, do it all for the glory of God." 1 Corinthians 10:31

Live to Thrive

To acquire wisdom is to love yourself; people who cherish
understanding will prosper.

Proverbs 19:8

My dad used to take our family to a small, sandy beach he found in Newport Harbor on the Southern California coast. As I remember it, the beach wasn't more than a hundred feet long, and half as wide. Homes sat on either side of it. A narrow wooden pier with a small floating dock stretched out a dozen yards or so from the beach into the harbor where sailboats and yachts passed by. Here was where I learned to swim.

I was 4 years old. I had a face mask to keep my eyes dry, a snorkel for breathing when my face was in the water, and a pair of blue fins to help my feet propel me. I'd wade slowly into the water until I was in up to my waist. Then I'd lean forward until my feet came off the bottom and my body was floating on the surface. I'd kick with my feet and paddle with my hands. Over time, I became confident enough to swim out to the dock, then back to the beach.

I taught myself to swim.

Starting Over

Fast forward to when I was 19. After a summer of working at Big Lake Youth Camp as a counselor, I wanted to work on the camp waterfront the next summer. To do that, I needed to get a Red Cross Water Safety Instructor certificate. I signed up for the course at the university as a freshman year elective.

I showed up for the first day of class at the indoor pool in my swim trunks. The instructor lined us up to swim laps. When it was my turn, I paddled with my hands and kicked with my feet. Those who knew what they were doing swam with a freestyle stroke. My stroke had more "free" than "style." My stroke wasn't much different than what I'd taught myself at 4 years old. By the end of the one lap, I was winded.

The instructor motioned me over to the side of the pool, and crouched at the edge.

"Are you ok?" she asked.

"Oh, yeah," I replied, out of breath.

"Have you ever had swimming lessons?"

"No," I confessed.

"I think you need to start over with swimming lessons before you take this course," she advised.

That day I dropped the Water Safety Instructor course and signed up for Intermediate Swimming.

I started the swimming class later that week, and over time learned the proper form for a freestyle stroke. I also learned the breast stroke, butterfly, sidestroke and backstroke. Outside of class I'd visit the pool to practice my strokes and build up my endurance. By the time the class ended, I'd made remarkable improvements in my swimming skill. I finished as one of the top swimmers in the class.

A few months after finishing the Intermediate Swimming class, I took private lessons from a friend to earn my Water Safety Instructor certification. That fall, I could barely swim a lap. By winter, I was a Water Safety Instructor and got a job as a lifeguard at the pool.

Before I started the first Water Safety Instructor course, I thought I knew how to swim. My eyes were opened. I stepped back, and got a new start. I learned what I needed to know. I practiced it. With time and effort, I didn't just learn how to swim–I excelled. I finished the second Water Safety Instructor course in two weeks.

It's Your Time to Thrive

Before reading this book, perhaps all you knew about how to live were things you'd learned in the school of hard knocks. Perhaps you picked up a few tips from your parents, or learned some things from friends and acquaintances. But, until now, you've only known how to survive.

Now you know how to thrive.

Now it's time to put what you've learned into practice. If you've already started, keep it up.

I encourage you to take these 7 habits for thriving in faith, relationships and work and practice them daily. Keep doing them until you do them without even thinking about it. Then they will have become habits.

It's your time to thrive. There will never be an easier time to begin than now. There will never be a better day to begin than today.

Start with one habit at a time, from the beginning. Don't start without receiving God's love. God's love is the energy that will empower you to flourish.

Don't Stand Alone

You're not alone.

A seedling that grows alongside the thick trunk of a mature tree stands a better chance of thriving than a seedling that sprouts from a seed dropped in the middle of a field of grass.

Don't stand alone.

If you ask Him, God walks with you to nourish you with love, shield you when you feel vulnerable, strengthen you when you feel weak, and pick you up when you fall.

Trees that grow in a forest stand stronger than a tree that grows alone.

Participate in communities of people who are alive to thrive, such as my Alive to Thrive tribe.

If you join my Alive to Thrive tribe, I'll encourage you. I'll help you live to thrive, so you can help others thrive. As a tribe member, you'll receive direct email access to me, free access to my weekly coaching emails, an invitation to my exclusive Facebook group where tribe members can encourage each other, and other special offers.

It's all designed to help you live to thrive.

Sign up for my Alive to Thrive tribe today at **www.jonbeaty.com/bonuses** and receive your free 1-page Alive to Thrive infographic to print and post in your bathroom, at your desk, or anywhere else it can serve as a reminder of the new life you want to live.

I also want to hear how you liked this book, and hope you'll post a review on Amazon at http://amzn.to/2cxb70k. Put the URL in your internet browser and scroll down to the reviews to add your own. I welcome your feedback, and hope you'll tell others about this book.

You're designed to thrive in your faith, relationships and work.

Now it's your turn.

Live to Thrive!

About the Author

Jon Beaty is a life coach, teacher, counselor, speaker and writer. For over 25 years, Jon has worked in mental health and substance abuse treatment clinics, and for international healthcare organizations helping people achieve better health and live to thrive. Jon is a licensed clinical social worker in the state of Oregon, and a certified professional in healthcare quality by the Healthcare Quality Certification Board.

In addition to this book, Jon's work has been published by:

- *Journal for Healthcare Quality*
- *Journal of Managed Care Medicine*
- *Journal of Nursing Care Quality*
- *Insight Magazine*
- *Signs of the Times*
- *The Good Men Project*
- *LifeZette*

Jon has also given presentations at conferences for the following organizations:

- World Research Group
- Health Intelligence Network

- National Institute for Case Management
- National Association for Healthcare Quality
- American Association of Health Plans

Jon is also a church leader, having chaired and served on boards, and served in various leadership positions.

Jon lives outside of Estacada, Oregon, near Portland, on a hobby farm. With his wife Tami, and their children, they raise Boer goats, provide homes for honeybees, and grow fruits and vegetables.

Jon's website and blog are located **www.jonbeaty.com.**

Made in the USA
Middletown, DE
25 February 2018